NAKED TOKYO

VOL.1

BATHTUB

BLACK & WHITE

CONFIDENCE

CONFIDENCE
?

CONFIDENCE
?

ANGER

EROTIQUE

HAPPYNESS

MYSTERIOUS

SAD

ON THE BED

THE END

www.ingramcontent.com/pod-product-compliance
Lightning Source LLC
Chambersburg PA
CBHW051916210526
45473CB00006B/2040